PANSY

BOTANICAL CHARACTERISTICS

Pansy, scientifically known as Viola tricolor, *is a flowering plant species belonging to the family Violaceae. It is a small herbaceous perennial that is commonly cultivated as an annual or biennial plant. Pansies are renowned for their vibrant and diverse colors, making them a popular choice for garden beds, borders, and containers.*

PHYSICAL APPEARANCE

The physical appearance of pansies can vary, but they typically have the following characteristics:

- Flowers: Pansy flowers are large and showy, consisting of five petals. The petals can be solid or adorned with intricate patterns and markings. The color range of pansy flowers is extensive, including shades of purple, yellow, blue, red, orange, and white. Some varieties exhibit a combination of two or more colors on a single flower.
- Foliage: Pansy leaves are green and have a distinctive heart or oval shape. They are slightly hairy and can grow in a rosette pattern at the base of the plant.
- Size: Pansy plants usually reach a height of 6-10 inches (15-25 centimeters) and spread to about 6-9 inches (15-23 centimeters) in width.

- **Growth Habit:** Pansies have a compact and bushy growth habit. Their stems are relatively short and may branch out, supporting multiple flowers.

Pansies are known for their cheerful and charming appearance, making them a delightful addition to gardens, flower beds, and even indoor spaces. Their distinct colors and patterns bring beauty and vibrancy to any landscape.

PANSY: DIFFERENT SPECIES AND VARIETIES

SPECIES

There are several species of pansies, each with its own unique characteristics. Here are a few notable species:

VIOLA TRICOLOR (WILD PANSY)

Also known as wild pansy or heartsease, Viola tricolor is the species from which modern garden pansies have been derived. It has small, delicate flowers with three distinct colors: purple, yellow, and white. Wild pansies are often found in meadows and grassy areas.

VARIETIES

Pansies have been extensively bred and hybridized, resulting in a wide range of varieties. Here are some popular pansy varieties:

DELTA SERIES

The Delta series is known for its large flowers and vibrant colors. These pansies exhibit excellent heat tolerance, making them suitable for both cool and mild climates.

CLEAR CRYSTALS SERIES

The Clear Crystals series features pansies with clear, intense colors and contrasting dark blotches on the petals. They are highly uniform in growth and have a compact habit.

UNIVERSAL SERIES

The Universal series pansies are characterized by their large flowers and sturdy stems. They come in a wide array of colors and have a long flowering period, making them a popular choice for garden displays.

MAJESTIC GIANT SERIES

As the name suggests, the Majestic Giant series pansies produce large, ruffled flowers that create a stunning visual impact. They are available in a variety of vibrant colors and are often used for showy bedding displays.

WINTER/SPRING-FLOWERING VARIETIES

There are also specific varieties of pansies bred for winter and early spring blooming. These varieties, such as the 'Crystal Bowl' series, 'Winter Fire' and 'Winter Lace,' are known for their cold tolerance and ability to withstand frost.

Pansies offer a vast selection of colors, patterns, and sizes, allowing gardeners to create beautiful displays and enjoy their charm throughout the seasons.

PANSY: POPULARITY AS A GARDEN PLANT AND LANDSCAPE USES

POPULARITY AS A GARDEN PLANT

Pansies have long been a beloved choice among gardeners for their numerous appealing qualities. Here's why they are popular as a garden plant:

COLORFUL AND VIBRANT DISPLAY

Pansies are renowned for their vibrant and diverse range of colors. From rich purples and blues to bright yellows, oranges, and reds, pansies offer a wide palette to add a burst of color to any garden or landscape. Their flowers can also feature captivating patterns and markings, enhancing their visual appeal.

ADAPTABILITY

Pansies are highly adaptable plants, capable of thriving in various growing conditions. They can tolerate both full sun and partial shade, making them versatile for different areas of the garden. Pansies are also able to withstand cooler temperatures, allowing for early spring or late fall planting and extended blooming seasons in temperate regions.

EASY TO GROW

Gardeners of all skill levels appreciate pansies for their ease of cultivation. These plants are generally low-maintenance and require minimal care. Pansies can be grown from seeds or purchased as young plants from nurseries, making them accessible to beginners. With proper watering and occasional deadheading, pansies can thrive and produce abundant blooms.

LANDSCAPE USES

Pansies offer numerous landscape uses, enhancing the beauty and functionality of outdoor spaces. Here are some common applications:

BEDDING PLANTS

Pansies are frequently used as bedding plants, creating stunning displays in flower beds and borders. Their compact growth habit and vibrant colors make them an excellent choice for adding visual interest to garden landscapes.

CONTAINER GARDENING

Due to their versatility and adaptability, pansies are popular choices for container gardening. They can be planted in pots, hanging baskets, or window boxes, allowing for portable displays of color on patios, balconies, and other outdoor living areas.

GROUND COVERS

Pansies can be utilized as ground covers in garden areas where a low-growing and spreading plant is desired. Their foliage forms a dense mat, suppressing weed growth and adding a carpet of colorful flowers to the landscape.

EDGING AND BORDER PLANTS

The neat and compact growth habit of pansies makes them well-suited for edging garden beds and borders. Their vibrant flowers serve as a delightful border along pathways, creating a visually appealing transition between different areas of the landscape.

Pansies' popularity as a garden plant stems from their stunning colors, adaptability, and ease of cultivation. Whether used as bedding plants, container displays, ground covers, or border plants, pansies bring beauty and charm to various landscape settings.

PANSY: CULTURAL SIGNIFICANCE IN VARIOUS SOCIETIES AND TRADITIONS

FOLKLORE AND SYMBOLISM

Pansies have held cultural significance in various societies and traditions, often associated with folklore, symbolism, and meanings. Here are some examples:

LOVE AND AFFECTION

In the language of flowers, pansies are often associated with love and affection. They symbolize heartfelt emotions, fondness, and admiration. In some traditions, giving pansies as a gift is believed to express romantic interest or to convey a message of loving thoughts.

REMEMBRANCE AND SOUVENIRS

Pansies have been associated with remembrance and souvenirs. In certain cultures, they are used to honor and remember loved ones who have passed away. Pansies may be planted or offered as floral tributes in memorial gardens or used in funeral arrangements as a symbol of remembrance and everlasting love.

VICTORIAN ERA LANGUAGE OF FLOWERS

During the Victorian era, the language of flowers was a popular way of communicating sentiments and messages through the use of specific flowers. Pansies held symbolic meanings during this period:

THOUGHTS AND MEMORIES

Pansies were often associated with thoughts and memories. They were seen as flowers that could inspire thoughtful contemplation and evoke cherished memories. Pansies were given as tokens of remembrance and were used in floral arrangements to convey heartfelt sentiments.

FREE THINKING AND NONCONFORMITY

Pansies were also associated with free thinking and nonconformity. Their unique and varied patterns were seen as a symbol of individuality and breaking away from societal norms. Pansies were sometimes worn or gifted to express a sense of rebellion or to show support for unconventional ideas.

REGIONAL TRADITIONS

Pansies have had specific cultural significance in various regions around the world:

JAPAN

In Japanese culture, pansies are often associated with the concept of hanakotoba, the language of flowers. Pansies are seen as flowers that bring happiness and joy. They are celebrated for their cheerful colors and are given as gifts to bring positive energy and good luck.

UNITED KINGDOM

In the United Kingdom, pansies have been traditionally associated with remembrance and the Poppy Day commemorations. Pansies are often worn alongside poppies to honor and remember fallen soldiers, particularly during Remembrance Day ceremonies.

Pansies' cultural significance in various societies and traditions highlights their connection to emotions, memories, individuality, and commemoration. Their symbolism and meanings have added depth and significance to the beauty of these enchanting flowers.

PANSY: CULTIVATION AND PROPAGATION

CULTIVATION REQUIREMENTS

Pansies are relatively easy to cultivate, and with proper care, they can thrive in a variety of gardening conditions. Here are some key aspects of pansy cultivation:

SUNLIGHT:

Pansies prefer cool temperatures and thrive in partial shade to full sun. They can tolerate a few hours of direct sunlight each day, especially in cooler climates. In regions with hot summers, providing them with some shade during the hottest parts of the day can help prevent stress and prolong their blooming period.

SOIL:

Well-draining soil is crucial for pansy cultivation. They prefer fertile soil that retains moisture without becoming waterlogged. Amending the soil with organic matter, such as compost, can improve its drainage and nutrient content.

WATERING:

Pansies have moderate water requirements. Water the plants consistently to keep the soil evenly moist, but avoid overwatering, as it can lead to root rot. Watering in the morning allows excess moisture to evaporate during the day and reduces the risk of fungal diseases.

FERTILIZATION:

Regular fertilization helps promote healthy growth and abundant blooming. Use a balanced, water-soluble fertilizer according to the manufacturer's instructions. Avoid excessive nitrogen, as it can promote foliage growth at the expense of flowers.

DEADHEADING:

Deadheading, or removing spent flowers, encourages continuous blooming and prevents seed formation. Pinch off the faded blooms at the base of the stem to promote the development of new buds and prolong the flowering season.

PROPAGATION

Pansies can be propagated through various methods. Here are the primary techniques:

SEEDS:

Seeds are the most common and economical way to propagate pansies. Start seeds indoors 8-10 weeks before the last frost date or sow them directly in the garden after the danger of frost has passed. Plant the seeds in well-prepared soil, lightly covering them with a thin layer of soil or vermiculite. Keep the soil moist and provide adequate light for germination.

TRANSPLANTS:

Transplants are readily available at nurseries and garden centers. These young pansy plants can be planted directly in the garden or used to fill containers or hanging baskets. Ensure that the transplants have been hardened off before planting them outdoors to acclimate them to outdoor conditions.

SELF-SEEDING:

Pansies are known to self-seed, meaning that if allowed, they can drop seeds that will germinate and grow new plants. This can lead to naturalized pansy patches in the garden. However, not all varieties produce viable self-seeding seeds, so it's best to collect and save seeds from desired varieties for intentional propagation.

By providing suitable growing conditions and choosing the appropriate propagation method, gardeners can *enjoy the beauty and charm of pansies in their gardens and landscapes.*

PANSY: IDEAL GROWING CONDITIONS AND SOIL REQUIREMENTS

IDEAL GROWING CONDITIONS

To ensure optimal growth and abundant blooming, pansies thrive in specific growing conditions. Here are the ideal conditions for cultivating pansies:

TEMPERATURE:

Pansies prefer cool temperatures ranging from 45°F to 65°F (7°C to 18°C). They thrive in regions with mild winters and cool spring or fall seasons. In warmer climates, pansies are often grown as winter or early spring flowers when temperatures are cooler.

SUNLIGHT:

Pansies perform best in partial shade to full sun. They require a minimum of 4-6 hours of direct sunlight each day, especially in regions with cooler climates. In hotter regions, providing some shade during the hottest part of the day can help prevent stress and prolong their blooming period.

AIR CIRCULATION:

Good air circulation is important for pansies to prevent fungal diseases. Avoid planting them in crowded or congested areas where air movement is restricted. This allows for proper ventilation and helps maintain plant health.

SOIL REQUIREMENTS

Pansies have specific soil requirements to ensure healthy growth and development. Here's what you need to know:

WELL-DRAINING SOIL:

Pansies prefer well-draining soil to prevent waterlogging, which can lead to root rot and other problems. The soil should allow excess moisture to drain freely while retaining enough moisture for the plants to thrive. Amending the soil with organic matter, such as compost, can help improve drainage and provide essential nutrients.

PH LEVEL:

Pansies prefer slightly acidic to neutral soil with a pH level between 5.5 and 7.0. Conduct a soil test to determine the pH of your soil and make necessary adjustments by adding amendments if needed. Maintaining the appropriate pH level helps optimize nutrient availability to the plants.

FERTILITY:

Pansies grow best in fertile soil that is rich in organic matter. Prior to planting, incorporate compost or well-rotted manure into the soil to enhance its fertility. This helps provide essential nutrients and promotes healthy growth and abundant blooming.

MOISTURE RETENTION:

Pansies require soil that retains some moisture without becoming waterlogged. The soil should have good water-holding capacity, allowing the plants to access moisture during dry periods. Regular watering is necessary to keep the soil evenly moist but avoid overwatering, which can lead to root diseases.

By providing the ideal growing conditions and ensuring proper soil requirements, gardeners can cultivate healthy and vibrant pansy plants that will delight with their colorful flowers.

PANSY: IMPACT OF CLIMATE CHANGE AND CONSERVATION EFFORTS

IMPACT OF CLIMATE CHANGE

Climate change poses several challenges to the growth and survival of pansies. Here are some impacts of climate change on this plant:

SHIFTED GROWING SEASONS:

Warmer temperatures and changing weather patterns associated with climate change can disrupt the traditional growing seasons for pansies. They may experience shorter periods of optimal growth and blooming or face challenges adapting to shifting temperature patterns.

EXTREME WEATHER EVENTS:

Climate change increases the frequency and intensity of extreme weather events such as heatwaves, droughts, and heavy rainfall. Pansies can be susceptible to damage or stress during these events, leading to reduced growth, flower loss, or increased vulnerability to diseases and pests.

ALTERED DISTRIBUTION PATTERNS:

As climate conditions change, the suitable habitats for pansies may shift. This can affect their natural distribution patterns and potentially lead to changes in their availability and population dynamics. Some pansy species or varieties may struggle to adapt to new climate conditions or face challenges in finding suitable habitats for growth and reproduction.

CONSERVATION EFFORTS

Conservation efforts are vital to protect and preserve the diversity and resilience of pansy populations. Here are some conservation initiatives and practices:

SEED BANKING:

Seed banks play a crucial role in conserving the genetic diversity of pansies. Seeds from various species and varieties are collected, stored, and cataloged for future use. This helps preserve the genetic material of pansies and ensures their availability for research, breeding programs, and ecosystem restoration efforts.

HABITAT CONSERVATION:

Protecting and restoring natural habitats where pansies occur is essential for their long-term conservation. This includes conserving meadows, grasslands, and other natural areas where wild pansy species thrive. *Preserving their native habitats helps maintain the ecological balance and supports the survival of pansy populations and the associated biodiversity.*

RESEARCH AND BREEDING:

Continued research and breeding efforts focus on developing pansy varieties that are more resilient to changing climatic conditions. This includes identifying traits such as heat and drought tolerance, disease resistance, and adaptability to new environments. These efforts aim to ensure the availability of pansy cultivars that can thrive and bloom successfully under future climate scenarios.

EDUCATION AND AWARENESS:

Increasing public awareness about the impacts of climate change on plants like pansies is crucial for fostering conservation efforts. Education programs, public campaigns, and community engagement initiatives help promote understanding and encourage individuals to take actions that reduce carbon emissions, conserve resources, and support the conservation of plant species in general.

Through proactive conservation measures and collective efforts, it is possible to mitigate the impact of

climate change on pansies and ensure their
preservation for future generations to enjoy.

PANSY: SEASONAL CARE AND MAINTENANCE

SPRING CARE

Spring is a crucial season for pansy care as it sets the stage for their growth and blooming. Here are some key care practices during spring:

PLANTING OR TRANSPLANTING:

In early spring, plant pansy transplants or sow seeds directly in the garden. Choose a location with partial shade to full sun and well-draining soil. Ensure the plants are properly spaced to allow for airflow and future growth.

WATERING:

Provide regular watering to keep the soil evenly moist. Water the plants at the base to avoid wetting the foliage, which can lead to fungal diseases. Adjust the frequency of watering based on weather conditions and soil moisture levels.

FERTILIZATION:

Apply a balanced, slow-release fertilizer to provide essential nutrients to the pansies. Follow the

*manufacturer's instructions for application rates.
Fertilize every 4-6 weeks throughout the growing
season to support healthy growth and abundant
blooming.*

SUMMER CARE

*Summer brings warmer temperatures and increased
care requirements for pansies. Here's how to care for
them during the summer months:*

WATERING:

*As temperatures rise, pansies may require more
frequent watering. Ensure the soil remains consistently
moist, but avoid overwatering. Mulching around the
plants can help retain soil moisture and reduce weed
growth.*

DEADHEADING:

*Regularly remove faded or spent flowers by pinching
them off at the base. Deadheading promotes
continuous blooming and prevents the formation of
seeds, allowing the plants to redirect their energy
towards new flower production.*

MONITORING FOR PESTS AND DISEASES:

Keep a close eye on the plants for any signs of pests or diseases. Common pests that may affect pansies include aphids, slugs, and snails. If necessary, take appropriate measures such as applying organic pest control methods or using insecticidal soap to manage infestations.

FALL CARE

Fall is a season of transition for pansies. Proper care during this time ensures their health and prepares them for the colder months. Here's what to do:

WATERING:

Continue to provide regular watering, ensuring the soil remains moist. Be mindful of decreasing daylight and cooler temperatures, adjusting the frequency of watering accordingly.

REMOVING SPENT PLANTS:

As pansies reach the end of their blooming period, consider removing them from the garden. This allows space for new plantings or prepares the bed for winter crops. If desired, save seeds from specific varieties for future propagation.

SOIL PREPARATION:

Before winter sets in, prepare the soil by incorporating organic matter, such as compost, into the planting area. This enriches the soil and improves its structure for future planting or for the following spring's pansy season.

By providing seasonal care and maintenance, pansies can thrive and reward gardeners with their beautiful blooms throughout the year.

PANSY: COMMON PESTS AND DISEASES

COMMON PESTS

APHIDS:

Aphids are small, soft-bodied insects that suck sap from pansy leaves and stems. They can cause curling or distortion of leaves and the presence of sticky honeydew. Use insecticidal soap or a strong spray of water to control aphid infestations.

SLUGS AND SNAILS:

Slugs and snails are nocturnal pests that feed on pansy leaves, leaving irregular holes and slimy trails. Set up traps or use natural deterrents like copper tape or diatomaceous earth to protect pansies from slugs and snails.

SPIDER MITES:

Spider mites are tiny pests that feed on the undersides of pansy leaves, causing stippling or yellowing. They spin fine webs and can rapidly reproduce in hot, dry conditions. Use insecticidal soap or neem oil to control spider mite infestations.

COMMON DISEASES

POWDERY MILDEW:

Powdery mildew is a fungal disease that appears as a white, powdery coating on the leaves of pansies. It thrives in humid conditions and can cause stunted growth and leaf distortion. Provide adequate spacing between plants, promote good airflow, and apply fungicidal sprays to prevent powdery mildew.

LEAF SPOT:

Leaf spot is a common fungal disease that causes dark, circular spots on pansy leaves. These spots may have a yellow halo and can lead to defoliation if severe. To manage leaf spot, remove and dispose of infected leaves, avoid overhead watering, and apply fungicidal treatments as needed.

CROWN ROT:

Crown rot is a fungal disease that affects the base of pansy plants, causing them to wilt, rot, and eventually die. It thrives in overly wet or poorly drained soil. To prevent crown rot, ensure proper soil drainage and avoid overwatering. Remove and destroy infected plants promptly.

Regular monitoring, early detection, and prompt action are key to managing pests and diseases in pansies.

Implementing good cultural practices such as proper watering, adequate spacing, and maintaining healthy soil conditions can help prevent many pest and disease issues.

PANSY: POTENTIAL BENEFITS FOR PETS AND ANIMALS

ATTRACTING POLLINATORS

Pansies, with their colorful and nectar-rich flowers, have the potential to attract various pollinators such as bees, butterflies, and hummingbirds. These pollinators play a crucial role in the ecosystem by aiding in the pollination of plants, which leads to the production of fruits, seeds, and a healthy plant population.

EDIBLE AND NUTRITIOUS FOR HERBIVOROUS PETS

Pansies are considered safe for consumption by herbivorous pets, such as rabbits and guinea pigs, in moderate amounts. However, it's important to ensure that the pansies have not been treated with pesticides or other chemicals that could be harmful to pets. Always consult with a veterinarian before introducing new foods to your pet's diet.

AESTHETICALLY PLEASING FOR OBSERVING PETS AND ANIMAL ENCLOSURES

Pansies, with their vibrant colors and compact growth habit, can provide visual interest and enrichment for observing pets and animals. Whether planted in a garden, used in containers, or placed in animal enclosures, pansies can create an aesthetically pleasing environment for pets and animals to enjoy.

NON-TOXIC TO CATS AND DOGS

Pansies are generally considered non-toxic to cats and dogs. While ingestion of pansies may cause mild gastrointestinal upset in pets, severe toxic reactions are unlikely. However, it's always recommended to monitor pets around plants and consult a veterinarian if any unusual symptoms occur.

THERAPEUTIC EFFECTS

Engaging with nature and plants can have therapeutic effects on both pets and their owners. The act of tending to pansies, observing their growth, and enjoying their beauty can provide a calming and stress-relieving experience. Pets and animals can benefit from the soothing and relaxing environment that pansies can create.

While pansies can offer potential benefits for pets and animals, it's important to consider individual sensitivities and consult with professionals, such as veterinarians or animal experts, to ensure the safety and well-being of the animals in question.

PANSY: SAFETY FOR KIDS AND HOME PETS

NON-TOXIC PLANT

Pansies are generally considered non-toxic to both kids and home pets, such as cats and dogs.

KIDS

NO KNOWN TOXICITY

Pansies are not known to contain any toxic compounds that pose a significant danger to children if accidentally ingested. However, it's always important to teach children about the potential risks of consuming any plants and to discourage them from eating any plant material unless supervised.

PETS

NO SEVERE TOXICITY

Pansies are generally safe for cats and dogs. While ingestion of pansies may cause mild gastrointestinal upset, such as vomiting or diarrhea, severe toxic reactions are unlikely.

Although pansies are considered non-toxic, it's important to take precautions to ensure the safety of home pets:

- Avoid using pesticides or chemicals on or around pansies that could be harmful if ingested by pets.
- Monitor pets around pansy plants to prevent excessive consumption, as large amounts of any plant material may lead to digestive issues.
- If you suspect your pet has ingested a large quantity of pansies or exhibits concerning symptoms, consult a veterinarian for guidance.

While pansies are generally safe, it's always a good idea to supervise children and pets when they are in contact with any plants to prevent potential issues.

PANSY: STAGES OF GROWTH AND DEVELOPMENT

SEED GERMINATION

When a pansy seed is provided with suitable conditions, such as moisture and warmth, it begins the process of germination.

SEED IMBIBITION

The seed absorbs water, causing it to swell and soften the outer seed coat.

ROOT AND SHOOT EMERGENCE

The seed sends out a primary root that anchors the plant into the soil. Meanwhile, the shoot emerges from the seed and begins to grow upward.

SEEDLING STAGE

As the pansy seedling continues to grow, it goes through several developmental phases.

LEAF DEVELOPMENT

The seedling produces its first set of true leaves, which look different from the initial seed leaves (cotyledons).

These true leaves resemble the mature pansy leaves in shape and characteristics.

ESTABLISHMENT OF ROOT SYSTEM

The root system continues to develop, branching out and growing deeper into the soil. This allows the plant to absorb water and nutrients more efficiently.

INCREASED SHOOT GROWTH

The shoot system continues to elongate, and additional leaves develop, contributing to the overall growth of the pansy seedling.

VEGETATIVE GROWTH

During this stage, the pansy plant focuses on leaf and stem development, preparing for future flowering.

LEAF EXPANSION

The leaves continue to expand in size, becoming more prominent and lush. This growth contributes to the overall vitality of the plant.

STEM ELONGATION

The stem continues to elongate, allowing the plant to reach its full height. This stage is essential for providing support to the developing flowers.

FLOWERING STAGE

As the pansy plant reaches maturity, it enters the flowering stage, where the vibrant and distinctive flowers begin to emerge.

FLOWER BUD FORMATION

The plant produces flower buds, which gradually develop and mature.

FULL BLOOM

The flower buds open up to reveal the characteristic pansy flowers, with their vibrant colors, distinct patterns, and delicate petals.

SEED PRODUCTION

After pollination, the pansy flowers produce seeds within seed capsules. These seeds can be collected for future propagation or allowed to disperse naturally.

Throughout its life cycle, from seed to mature plant, the pansy undergoes distinct stages of growth and development, culminating in the production of beautiful flowers.

PANSY: ROLE IN LANDSCAPING AND GARDEN DESIGN

COLORFUL BLOOMS

Pansies are highly valued for their colorful blooms, which make them a popular choice in landscaping and garden design.

SEASONAL INTEREST

Pansies provide vibrant blooms in a wide range of colors, including shades of purple, yellow, orange, red, pink, and white. Their flowers add a splash of color to gardens and landscapes, creating visual interest and enhancing the overall aesthetics.

FLORAL DISPLAYS

Pansies can be used to create stunning floral displays, either as standalone plantings or in combination with other flowering plants. They work well in beds, borders, containers, hanging baskets, and window boxes, adding charm and beauty to various garden settings.

VERSATILE PLANTING OPTIONS

Pansies offer versatility in garden design, allowing for a wide range of creative planting options.

MASS PLANTINGS

Pansies can be mass-planted to create vibrant and eye-catching displays. Planting them in large groups or drifts can produce a striking visual impact, particularly when different colors or varieties are combined.

EDGING AND BORDERS

Pansies work well as edging plants or in border plantings. Their low-growing and compact habit makes them suitable for defining pathways, borders, or garden beds, adding a neat and colorful edge to the landscape.

CONTAINER GARDENING

Pansies thrive in containers, making them an excellent choice for container gardening. They can be planted in pots, hanging baskets, or window boxes, allowing for flexibility in design and placement. Pansies can bring color and beauty to porches, patios, balconies, and other outdoor spaces.

SEASONAL TRANSITIONS

Pansies play a role in bridging the gap between seasons and adding interest during transitional periods.

WINTER GARDENING

Pansies are known for their cold tolerance, making them a popular choice for winter gardening. They can withstand frost and continue to bloom during milder winter climates, providing color and life to gardens when other plants may be dormant.

SPRING AND FALL PLANTINGS

Pansies are often used for spring and fall plantings, as they thrive in cooler temperatures. They can be planted alongside other seasonal flowers to create beautiful displays and extend the flowering season.

With their vibrant blooms, versatility, and ability to thrive in various conditions, pansies are valued for their role in landscaping and garden design, allowing for creative expression and adding beauty to outdoor spaces.

PANSY: DIFFERENT USES IN GARDENING

BEDDING PLANTS

Pansies are commonly used as bedding plants in gardens and landscapes.

COLORFUL DISPLAYS

Planted in flower beds or mass plantings, pansies create vibrant and eye-catching displays with their colorful blooms. They can be arranged in patterns or mixed with other flowering plants to create beautiful and dynamic bedding designs.

SEASONAL INTEREST

Pansies are well-suited for seasonal bedding displays, providing color and interest during spring, fall, and even winter in milder climates. Their ability to withstand cooler temperatures makes them valuable for maintaining garden beauty throughout the year.

CUT FLOWERS

Pansies are also used as cut flowers, bringing their charm indoors and adding a touch of beauty to floral arrangements.

SMALL BOUQUETS AND ARRANGEMENTS

Pansy blooms, with their delicate petals and vibrant colors, can be cut and incorporated into small bouquets and floral arrangements. They add a whimsical and charming element to indoor decorations, whether used alone or combined with other flowers.

TABLETOP DECORATIONS

Pansies can be floated in shallow bowls or used to adorn tabletop centerpieces, adding a fresh and natural element to table decorations. Their colorful presence brings joy and liveliness to any indoor setting.

CONTAINER PLANTS

Pansies are well-suited for container gardening, offering versatility and beauty in various types of containers.

POTS AND PLANTERS

Pansies can be planted in pots, planters, and window boxes, allowing for flexibility in design and placement. They thrive in containers, making them perfect for adding color to patios, balconies, porches, and other outdoor spaces.

HANGING BASKETS

Pansies are commonly used in hanging baskets, where their trailing habit and vibrant blooms spill over the edges, creating cascades of color. Hanging baskets filled with pansies can add visual interest and charm to vertical spaces.

Whether used as bedding plants to create colorful displays, cut flowers to enhance indoor arrangements, or container plants to beautify outdoor spaces, pansies offer a range of uses in gardening, allowing for creative expression and the enjoyment of their delightful blooms.

PANSY: PRESERVING AND DRYING METHODS FOR DECORATIVE PURPOSES

AIR DRYING

Air drying is a simple and effective method for preserving pansies and other flowers for decorative purposes.

HARVESTING

Choose pansies that are fully open and free from any signs of damage or disease. Harvest them in the morning when the flowers are at their freshest.

BUNDLING

Gather a small bunch of pansies and secure the stems together with a rubber band or a piece of string. Ensure the bunch is not too large to allow proper airflow.

HANGING

Hang the bundled pansies upside down in a dark, well-ventilated area. This will help preserve the flowers' shape and color as they dry. Ensure they are hung in a location away from direct sunlight and humidity.

DRYING TIME

It may take a few weeks for the pansies to fully dry. Once they are dry to the touch and the petals feel crisp, they are ready for decorative use.

PRESSED FLOWERS

Pressing pansies is another method of preserving their delicate beauty for decorative purposes.

PREPARATION

Select pansies with flat, undamaged petals. Remove any excess foliage and trim the stems short.

PRESSING

Place the pansies between layers of absorbent paper, such as blotting paper or parchment paper. Press the layers together tightly and place heavy objects, like books or a flower press, on top to apply pressure.

DRYING TIME

Leave the pansies pressed for a few weeks to allow them to dry completely. The flowers will flatten and retain their color, making them suitable for decorative purposes.

SILICA GEL DRYING

Silica gel is a desiccant that can be used to dry and preserve pansies quickly while maintaining their shape and color.

PREPARATION

Fill a container with a layer of silica gel, deep enough to accommodate the pansies without touching the bottom.

ARRANGING

Place the pansies carefully on the layer of silica gel, making sure the petals are spread out and not touching each other.

COVERING

Completely cover the pansies with more silica gel, ensuring they are fully surrounded. Gently tap the container to settle the gel around the flowers.

DRYING TIME

Seal the container with a lid and leave it undisturbed for several days. The silica gel will absorb moisture from the pansies, drying them while preserving their form and color.

By using air drying, pressing, or silica gel drying methods, pansies can be preserved and dried effectively, allowing you to enjoy their beauty in decorative arrangements, crafts, and other creative projects.

PANSY: HYBRIDIZATION AND BREEDING TECHNIQUES FOR CREATING NEW PLANT VARIETIES

HYBRIDIZATION

Hybridization is a common technique used in the breeding of pansies to create new plant varieties with desirable traits.

CROSS-POLLINATION

Hybridization involves cross-pollinating two different pansy plants with desired characteristics. This is typically done by transferring pollen from the stamen of one plant to the stigma of another plant.

SELECTION

After cross-pollination, the resulting seeds are collected from the parent plants. These seeds will give rise to offspring with a combination of traits from both parents.

EVALUATION

The resulting seedlings are evaluated for the desired traits, such as flower color, size, pattern, growth habit, and disease resistance. Only the seedlings that exhibit the desired characteristics are selected for further breeding.

BREEDING TECHNIQUES

Breeders use various techniques to further refine and develop new pansy varieties with specific traits.

SELECTIVE BREEDING

Selective breeding involves choosing plants with desirable traits from each generation and crossing them to consolidate and enhance those traits. This process is repeated over several generations to stabilize the desired characteristics.

BACKCROSSING

Backcrossing is a technique used to introduce specific traits from one parent plant into the offspring. It involves crossing the offspring back with one of the parent plants to reinforce and retain the desired traits while reducing the influence of unwanted traits.

MUTATION BREEDING

Mutation breeding involves exposing pansy plants to radiation or chemical mutagens to induce genetic mutations. These mutations can lead to the development of new and unique traits, which can then be selected and bred for in subsequent generations.

TISSUE CULTURE

Tissue culture is a laboratory-based technique used to propagate plants from small pieces of plant tissue. It allows for the rapid multiplication of selected pansy varieties and the production of genetically identical plants with desirable traits.

Through hybridization and breeding techniques, breeders can create new pansy varieties that possess a combination of desirable traits, including unique colors, patterns, sizes, and disease resistance. These techniques play a vital role in the ongoing development and improvement of pansy cultivars, providing a diverse range of options for gardeners and horticultural enthusiasts.

PANSY: ROLE IN TRADITIONAL MEDICINAL PRACTICES AND HERBAL REMEDIES

TRADITIONAL MEDICINAL USES

Pansies have been utilized in traditional medicinal practices for their potential health benefits.

RESPIRATORY HEALTH

Pansies have been used in herbal remedies to support respiratory health. Infusions or teas made from the flowers were believed to provide relief for coughs, sore throats, and respiratory congestion.

SKIN CONDITIONS

In traditional medicine, pansies were used topically to address various skin conditions. The flowers were believed to have soothing properties and were applied to skin irritations, rashes, and minor wounds.

ANTI-INFLAMMATORY PROPERTIES

Some traditional remedies utilized pansies for their potential anti-inflammatory effects. Pansy preparations were used externally to reduce inflammation and promote healing.

HERBAL REMEDIES

Pansies have also been incorporated into herbal remedies for their potential therapeutic properties.

TEAS AND INFUSIONS

Infusions or teas made from pansy flowers were traditionally used to prepare herbal remedies. The flowers were steeped in hot water to extract their beneficial compounds, and the resulting infusion was consumed for its potential medicinal effects.

SUPPORTING WELLNESS

In herbal medicine, pansies were believed to have overall tonic and wellness-supporting properties. They were used to promote general health and vitality, and to support the body's natural healing processes.

TRADITIONAL FORMULATIONS

Pansies were often combined with other herbs and botanical ingredients in traditional formulations to create remedies targeting specific ailments or health concerns.

It's important to note that the traditional uses of pansies in medicinal practices are based on historical beliefs and anecdotal evidence. While pansies may possess certain bioactive compounds, further scientific research is needed to validate their effectiveness and safety for specific medicinal applications.

Always consult with a healthcare professional or qualified herbalist before using pansies or any other botanical for medicinal purposes.

PANSY: CHALLENGES AND COMMON MISTAKES IN GROWING THE PLANT

CHALLENGES IN GROWING PANSIES

Growing pansies can come with a few challenges that gardeners may encounter.

TEMPERATURE EXTREMES

Pansies prefer cool temperatures and may struggle in regions with extremely hot summers. High temperatures can cause wilting, reduced flower production, and even plant death. On the other hand, severe winter frosts can also damage pansies. Providing appropriate temperature management is crucial for successful growth.

POOR DRAINAGE

Pansies require well-draining soil to prevent waterlogged roots, which can lead to root rot and other diseases. Poor drainage can be an issue, particularly in heavy clay soils. Ensuring proper soil preparation and adding organic matter can help improve drainage.

PEST INFESTATIONS

Common garden pests, such as aphids, slugs, and snails, can attack pansies and cause damage to leaves and flowers. Regular monitoring and implementing pest control measures, such as handpicking or using organic pest deterrents, can help prevent or minimize infestations.

COMMON MISTAKES IN GROWING PANSIES

INADEQUATE SUNLIGHT

Pansies require sufficient sunlight to thrive. Planting them in areas with insufficient light can result in weak growth, poor flowering, and leggy plants. Ensure pansies receive at least 4-6 hours of direct sunlight daily for optimal performance.

OVERWATERING OR UNDERWATERING

Watering pansies can be a delicate balance. Overwatering can lead to root rot and other fungal diseases, while underwatering can cause wilting and stunted growth. It's essential to provide consistent moisture by watering when the top inch of soil feels dry, ensuring the soil is evenly moist but not waterlogged.

NEGLECTING FERTILIZATION

Failure to provide adequate nutrients can result in weak, pale plants with poor flower production. Regularly fertilize pansies with a balanced, water-soluble fertilizer according to the recommended dosage to promote healthy growth and abundant blooms.

OVERCOMING CHALLENGES AND AVOIDING MISTAKES

To overcome challenges and avoid common mistakes in growing pansies, consider the following tips:

RESEARCH AND PLANNING

Understand the specific requirements of pansies and plan accordingly. Research their preferred growing conditions, including temperature ranges, sunlight needs, and soil requirements.

PROPER SITE SELECTION

Choose a well-drained location with adequate sunlight for planting pansies. Prepare the soil by incorporating organic matter and ensuring good drainage.

REGULAR MONITORING

Monitor your pansies regularly for signs of pest infestations, diseases, or nutrient deficiencies. Early detection allows for prompt intervention and prevention of further damage.

APPROPRIATE WATERING

Water pansies carefully, ensuring the soil remains consistently moist but not waterlogged. Adjust watering frequency based on weather conditions and plant needs.

CORRECT FERTILIZATION

Follow the recommended fertilization schedule and use a balanced fertilizer to provide the necessary nutrients for healthy growth and vibrant blooms.

By addressing these challenges and avoiding common mistakes, you can increase your success in growing pansies and enjoy their beautiful flowers throughout the growing season.

PANSY: CHALLENGES IN CONSERVATION AND PRESERVATION

HABITAT LOSS

The conservation and preservation of pansies face several challenges, with habitat loss being a significant concern.

URBANIZATION AND LAND DEVELOPMENT

The conversion of natural habitats for urbanization and land development reduces the available space for pansies to grow in their native environments. This loss of habitat can lead to a decline in wild populations and limit their ability to reproduce and persist in the long term.

INVASIVE SPECIES

Invasive species pose a threat to the conservation of pansies and their natural habitats.

COMPETITION FOR RESOURCES

Invasive plant species can outcompete pansies for essential resources such as water, nutrients, and sunlight. This competition can negatively impact the

growth and survival of pansies, leading to a decline in
their populations.

GENETIC POLLUTION

Invasive species can hybridize with native pansies,
resulting in genetic pollution. This can alter the genetic
makeup of native pansy populations and lead to the
loss of unique genetic diversity.

CLIMATE CHANGE

Climate change poses significant challenges to the
conservation of pansies and other plant species.

SHIFTS IN SUITABLE HABITATS

As temperatures and precipitation patterns change, the
suitable habitats for pansies may shift or become
fragmented. This can disrupt their natural distribution
and limit their ability to adapt and survive in new
environmental conditions.

ALTERED PHENOLOGY

Climate change can disrupt the timing of key events in
the pansy's life cycle, such as flowering and seed
production. Mismatches between the availability of
pollinators and the timing of pansy flowering can

reduce reproductive success and impact population dynamics.

CONSERVATION EFFORTS

Despite the challenges, conservation efforts are underway to preserve pansy species and protect their habitats.

HABITAT PRESERVATION

Efforts are being made to identify and protect important pansy habitats through the establishment of protected areas, conservation easements, and land management practices that prioritize their preservation.

INVASIVE SPECIES CONTROL

Management strategies are being implemented to control invasive species and reduce their negative impact on pansy populations. This includes the removal of invasive plants and the restoration of native plant communities.

SEED BANKS AND EX SITU CONSERVATION

Seed banks play a crucial role in the conservation of pansies by preserving their genetic diversity. Seeds are collected, stored, and maintained under controlled *conditions to ensure their long-term viability. Ex situ conservation efforts also include growing pansies in botanical gardens and arboreta for research, education, and species recovery programs.*

It is essential to continue monitoring pansy populations, conducting research on their biology and ecology, and raising awareness about the importance of conserving these plants. Collaborative efforts involving government agencies, conservation organizations, and local communities are vital for the long-term conservation and preservation of pansies and their natural habitats.

PANSY: SYMBOLISM IN WEDDINGS AND CELEBRATIONS

SYMBOLIC MEANINGS

Pansies hold symbolic significance in weddings and celebrations, representing various meanings and emotions.

LOVE AND AFFECTION

Pansies are often associated with love and affection, symbolizing the deep feelings and emotions shared between individuals. They can be used to express love, admiration, and fondness.

UNITY AND PARTNERSHIP

In weddings, pansies can represent unity and partnership, signifying the coming together of two individuals in a committed relationship. They symbolize the bond and harmony shared by the couple as they embark on their journey together.

REMEMBRANCE AND FOND MEMORIES

Pansies are also seen as a symbol of remembrance and fond memories. They can be included in wedding bouquets or decorations as a way to honor and remember loved ones who are no longer present.

WEDDING AND CELEBRATION USES

Pansies can be incorporated in various ways during weddings and celebratory events, adding beauty and symbolic significance to the occasion.

BOUQUETS AND FLORAL ARRANGEMENTS

Pansies can be included in bridal bouquets, bridesmaid bouquets, and other floral arrangements, adding color and charm. They can be mixed with other flowers or used as the main focal point, depending on the desired aesthetic.

CENTERPIECES AND DECORATIONS

Pansies can be used as centerpieces on reception tables, adding a touch of beauty and symbolism to the celebration. They can also be incorporated into floral decorations, such as wreaths, garlands, and arches, creating a festive atmosphere.

WEDDING FAVORS AND GIFTS

Pansies can be included as part of wedding favors or given as gifts to guests, symbolizing love, appreciation, and lasting memories. They can be presented as potted plants, seeds, or dried flower arrangements.

PERSONALIZED SYMBOLISM

While pansies have traditional symbolic meanings, their symbolism can also be personalized to reflect the unique characteristics and values of the couple or the celebratory event. The colors of pansies can be chosen to align with the wedding theme or to convey specific emotions.

It's important to note that the symbolic meanings of pansies may vary across cultures and individual interpretations. Their symbolism in weddings and celebrations is often influenced by personal beliefs and traditions.

By incorporating pansies into weddings and celebrations, individuals can add a touch of symbolism and beauty, infusing their special occasions with love, unity, and cherished memories.

PANSY: ROLE IN BIODIVERSITY CONSERVATION AND CONTRIBUTION TO LOCAL ECOSYSTEMS

IMPORTANCE IN BIODIVERSITY CONSERVATION

Pansies play a significant role in biodiversity conservation by contributing to the diversity and health of local ecosystems.

NATIVE PLANT SPECIES

As native plant species, pansies are adapted to the local environment and have evolved alongside other organisms in the ecosystem. By preserving and promoting the growth of pansies, we help maintain the natural balance and biodiversity of native plant communities.

HABITAT PROVISION

Pansies provide essential habitat and resources for various organisms, including insects, birds, and small mammals. They serve as a food source, offer shelter, and support the life cycles of many pollinators, such as bees and butterflies.

SUPPORTING POLLINATORS

Pansies play a crucial role in supporting pollinators, which are essential for ecosystem health and food production.

POLLINATOR-FRIENDLY FLOWERS

The vibrant and nectar-rich flowers of pansies attract a wide range of pollinators, including bees, butterflies, and hoverflies. These insects visit the flowers to feed on nectar and inadvertently transfer pollen from one flower to another, facilitating the pollination process.

ENHANCING POLLINATION SERVICES

By supporting pollinators, pansies contribute to the pollination of other plant species in the ecosystem. This cross-pollination helps ensure the reproduction and genetic diversity of various plant populations, contributing to overall ecosystem resilience.

EROSION CONTROL AND SOIL HEALTH

Pansies can also play a role in erosion control and maintaining soil health in local ecosystems.

ROOT SYSTEMS AND GROUND COVER

The root systems of pansies help stabilize the soil, preventing erosion in areas prone to runoff or wind.

Their dense foliage forms a ground cover that protects the soil from direct impact, reducing erosion caused by heavy rain or wind.

SOIL ENRICHMENT

Pansies contribute organic matter to the soil through leaf litter and root decay, enhancing soil fertility and nutrient cycling. This enrichment benefits other plant species and microorganisms in the ecosystem.

PROMOTING LOCAL BIODIVERSITY

By supporting the growth and conservation of pansies, we contribute to the preservation of local biodiversity and the interconnectedness of species in the ecosystem.

SPECIES INTERACTIONS

Pansies interact with other organisms in the ecosystem, forming complex ecological relationships. These interactions, such as pollination and seed dispersal, are vital for the survival and reproduction of various plant and animal species.

FOOD WEB SUPPORT

Pansies provide a source of food and resources for herbivores, omnivores, and predators within the local food web. They contribute to the intricate network of species interactions that sustain the biodiversity and ecological balance of the ecosystem.

By recognizing the role of pansies in biodiversity conservation and actively preserving their habitats, we contribute to the overall health and resilience of local ecosystems, supporting a thriving and diverse array of plant and animal life.

PANSY: TRADITIONAL USES IN BEAUTY AND COSMETICS

HISTORICAL SIGNIFICANCE

Pansies have a rich history of traditional use in beauty and cosmetics, with their vibrant flowers and various properties being utilized for different purposes.

ANCIENT BEAUTY PRACTICES

In ancient times, pansies were valued for their aesthetic appeal and were incorporated into beauty rituals and adornments by different cultures. The petals and extracts of pansies were used to enhance beauty and promote well-being.

SKINCARE BENEFITS

Pansies possess certain properties that make them beneficial for skincare and cosmetic applications.

SOOTHING AND MOISTURIZING

Pansies contain natural compounds that have soothing and moisturizing effects on the skin. They can help alleviate dryness, calm irritated skin, and promote a healthy complexion.

ANTI-INFLAMMATORY PROPERTIES

Extracts from pansies may have anti-inflammatory properties, which can help reduce redness and inflammation on the skin. This makes them useful in soothing sensitive or reactive skin.

TRADITIONAL USES

Pansies were traditionally incorporated into beauty and cosmetic preparations in various ways.

FACIAL STEAM AND COMPRESS

The petals of pansies were sometimes used in facial steams or compresses to refresh and revitalize the skin. The steam or compress allowed the beneficial compounds of the pansy to be absorbed by the skin, promoting a healthy complexion.

INFUSED OILS AND EXTRACTS

Pansy flowers were often infused in oils or used to create extracts, which were then incorporated into skincare products. These infused oils and extracts were believed to provide nourishment and improve the overall appearance of the skin.

COSMETIC APPLICATIONS

Pansy petals were sometimes used as a natural pigment in cosmetics, providing a touch of color to various beauty preparations. The vibrant and diverse colors of pansies made them a desirable choice for adding natural hues to cosmetics such as lip balms, blushes, or eyeshadows.

MODERN APPLICATION

While the traditional use of pansies in beauty and cosmetics may have evolved over time, their natural properties and aesthetic appeal continue to inspire modern skincare and cosmetic formulations.

NATURAL SKINCARE PRODUCTS

Pansy extracts and infusions are still utilized in some natural skincare products, offering gentle and soothing benefits for the skin. They can be found in creams, lotions, serums, and facial masks, providing moisturization, soothing effects, and support for overall skin health.

BOTANICAL COSMETICS

The vibrant colors of pansies continue to inspire the creation of botanical cosmetics. Some cosmetic brands incorporate natural pigments derived from pansy petals into their makeup products, offering an alternative to synthetic colorants.

It's important to note that while pansies have traditional uses in beauty and cosmetics, individual sensitivities and allergies may vary. As with any cosmetic product, it's advisable to perform a patch test and consult with a dermatologist or healthcare professional before using products containing pansy extracts or other botanical ingredients.

Overall, the traditional uses of pansies in beauty and cosmetics highlight their aesthetic appeal and beneficial properties, inspiring natural and botanical approaches to skincare and cosmetic formulations.

PANSY: CULINARY USES IN FOOD AND BEVERAGES

EDIBLE FLOWERS

Pansy flowers are not only visually appealing but also edible, adding a unique touch to culinary creations. Their vibrant colors and delicate flavor make them suitable for various culinary uses.

GARNISHES AND DECORATIONS

Pansy flowers are often used as decorative elements in salads, desserts, and drinks. They can be used whole or as individual petals, adding a splash of color and an elegant touch to the presentation of dishes.

CAKES AND BAKED GOODS

Pansies can be used to adorn cakes, cupcakes, and other baked goods, providing a visually appealing and edible decoration. They can be placed on top of frosting or pressed gently onto the surface of baked goods for a charming and natural embellishment.

INFUSIONS AND FLAVORED BEVERAGES

Pansies can also be used to infuse beverages, imparting their delicate flavor and creating visually enticing drinks.

HERBAL TEAS

Pansy flowers and leaves can be dried and used to make herbal teas. The infusion of pansies produces a mild and floral flavor, making it a soothing and aromatic beverage option.

INFUSED WATER AND COCKTAILS

Pansy flowers can be added to water or used as an ingredient in cocktails to infuse subtle flavors and create visually appealing beverages. The addition of pansies adds a touch of elegance and botanical essence to the drinks.

SALADS AND SAVORY DISHES

Pansy flowers can be incorporated into salads and savory dishes, lending their gentle flavor and visual appeal to culinary creations.

SALAD GARNISHES

Pansy flowers can be used as a decorative element in salads, adding color and texture to the dish. They can *be scattered on top of the salad or used as a focal point for presentation.*

SAVORY RECIPES

Pansies can be used as a unique ingredient in savory recipes, such as vegetable stir-fries or grain salads. Their delicate flavor complements various savory flavors, offering a subtle floral note to the dish.

When using pansies in culinary applications, it's important to ensure that the flowers are pesticide-free and suitable for consumption. If not growing your own pansies, it's advisable to source them from reputable suppliers who specialize in edible flowers.

The culinary uses of pansies allow for creativity and exploration in the kitchen, elevating dishes and beverages with their vibrant colors, delicate flavors, and charming presence.

PINKS: TRADITIONAL USES IN BEAUTY AND COSMETICS

HISTORICAL SIGNIFICANCE

Pinks, also known as Dianthus, have a long history of traditional use in beauty and cosmetics, with their aromatic flowers and various properties being valued for different purposes.

ANCIENT BEAUTY PRACTICES

In ancient times, pinks were highly regarded for their fragrance and were incorporated into beauty rituals and adornments by different cultures. The petals and extracts of pinks were used to enhance beauty and promote well-being.

SKINCARE BENEFITS

Pinks possess certain properties that make them beneficial for skincare and cosmetic applications.

ASTRINGENT AND SOOTHING

The petals and extracts of pinks contain natural compounds that have astringent and soothing effects on the skin. They can help tone and tighten the skin, reducing the appearance of pores and promoting a youthful complexion.

FRAGRANT ADDITIONS

The fragrance of pinks has been valued for its pleasant aroma. The scent of pinks is often used in perfumes, soaps, and other beauty products, adding a delightful and aromatic element.

TRADITIONAL USES

Pinks were traditionally incorporated into beauty and cosmetic preparations in various ways.

FACIAL TONERS AND MISTS

The petals and extracts of pinks were used to create facial toners and mists, which were applied to the skin to provide a refreshing and toning effect. These preparations were believed to help cleanse the skin and maintain its natural balance.

FRAGRANT BATHS AND SOAPS

Pinks were often added to baths or used in soap-making to infuse the water or soap with their delightful fragrance. These aromatic bathing rituals were considered luxurious and indulgent, providing a sensory experience.

MODERN APPLICATION

While the traditional use of pinks in beauty and cosmetics may have evolved over time, their natural properties and alluring fragrance continue to inspire modern skincare and cosmetic formulations.

FRAGRANCE AND PERFUME INDUSTRY

The unique and captivating scent of pinks is still highly valued in the perfume industry. The fragrance of pinks can be found in various perfumes, colognes, and scented products, offering a floral and uplifting aroma.

NATURAL SKINCARE PRODUCTS

Pinks and their extracts are often used in natural skincare products, such as creams, lotions, and serums. Their astringent properties and delightful fragrance make them a desirable ingredient in formulations aimed at toning and rejuvenating the skin.

It's important to note that while pinks have traditional uses in beauty and cosmetics, individual sensitivities and allergies may vary. As with any cosmetic product, it's advisable to perform a patch test and consult with a dermatologist or healthcare professional before using products containing pinks or other botanical ingredients.

The traditional uses of pinks in beauty and cosmetics highlight their aromatic allure and potential benefits, inspiring natural and fragrant approaches to skincare and cosmetic formulations.

PANSY: MYTHS AND LEGENDS IN DIFFERENT CULTURES

SYMBOLISM AND FOLKLORE

Pansies have captured the imagination of various cultures throughout history, giving rise to myths, legends, and symbolic interpretations.

A MESSENGER OF LOVE AND REMEMBRANCE

In some cultures, pansies are believed to be messengers of love and remembrance. They are associated with sentimental emotions, and their delicate appearance is often linked to expressions of affection and fond memories.

GREEK MYTHOLOGY

In Greek mythology, the pansy has a connection to the god of love, Eros, and his mother Aphrodite, the goddess of beauty and love.

THE LEGEND OF LOVE'S FLOWER

According to a Greek legend, the first pansy bloomed when Eros shot one of his arrows at a beautiful nymph, but missed, causing the arrow to hit a nearby violet instead. As a result, the violet transformed into a pansy, symbolizing the power of love.

CHRISTIAN SYMBOLISM

In Christian symbolism, pansies hold associations with religious figures and events.

REMEMBRANCE OF THE PASSION OF CHRIST

In Christian traditions, pansies are sometimes called "Hearts-ease" or "Trinity Flower." They are believed to represent the Holy Trinity, with the three colors of the pansy flower symbolizing the Father, the Son, and the Holy Spirit. Pansies were also associated with the passion of Christ, and their three lower petals were said to resemble the wounds of Christ on the cross.

VICTORIAN LANGUAGE OF FLOWERS

During the Victorian era, flowers were assigned specific meanings, and pansies were no exception.

REMEMBRANCE AND LOVING THOUGHTS

In the Victorian language of flowers, pansies were associated with remembrance and loving thoughts. They were often exchanged as tokens of affection, and their different colors conveyed specific sentiments, such as purple for loving thoughts, yellow for friendship, and white for innocence.

SUPERSTITIONS AND FOLK BELIEFS

In various folk beliefs and superstitions, pansies were thought to possess mystical properties and were associated with divination and luck.

DIVINATION AND LOVE CHARMS

In some folk traditions, it was believed that carrying or wearing pansies could enhance psychic abilities and facilitate divination. Pansies were also sometimes used in love charms or potions to attract love and enhance romantic relationships.

The myths, legends, and symbolism surrounding pansies in different cultures showcase the enduring allure and enchantment associated with this delicate flower.

PANSY: AROMATHERAPY AND THE USE OF PANSY IN SCENTED PREPARATIONS

AROMATHERAPY AND PANSY

Aromatherapy harnesses the therapeutic properties of aromatic plants, including pansies, to promote physical and emotional well-being. Pansies can be used in various forms in aromatherapy practices.

ESSENTIAL OILS

Pansy essential oil is derived from the flowers of the plant through a distillation process. The oil captures the unique fragrance and therapeutic compounds of the pansy.

METHODS OF USE

Pansy essential oil can be used in different ways in aromatherapy to enjoy its benefits.

AROMATHERAPY DIFFUSION

Adding a few drops of pansy essential oil to an aromatherapy diffuser or oil burner allows the gentle aroma of the flower to permeate the space. This method can create a soothing and relaxing ambiance, promoting a sense of calm and tranquility.

AROMATHERAPY MASSAGE

Pansy essential oil can be diluted in a carrier oil, such as jojoba or sweet almond oil, and used for aromatherapy massage. The oil blend can be gently massaged into the skin, providing a relaxing and aromatic experience.

AROMATHERAPY BATH

Adding a few drops of pansy essential oil to a warm bath can create a fragrant and therapeutic soak. The aroma of the oil can help uplift the spirits and enhance relaxation during the bathing experience.

AROMATHERAPY BENEFITS

The use of pansy in aromatherapy is associated with several potential benefits.

CALMING AND RELAXING

The delicate fragrance of pansy essential oil is known for its calming properties. Inhaling the aroma can help alleviate stress, anxiety, and promote relaxation.

MOOD ENHANCEMENT

The scent of pansy is often described as soothing and uplifting. Aromatherapy with pansy essential oil may help improve mood and create a positive atmosphere.

AROMATHERAPY BLENDING

Pansy essential oil can be blended with other essential oils to create customized aromatherapy blends. Combining it with oils such as lavender, bergamot, or geranium can enhance its therapeutic effects and create unique aromatic experiences.

When using pansy essential oil or any other essential oil for aromatherapy, it's important to follow proper dilution guidelines, perform patch tests, and consult with a qualified aromatherapist or healthcare professional for appropriate usage instructions.

Exploring pansy in aromatherapy allows for the integration of its fragrant essence into wellness practices, creating a sensory experience that promotes relaxation and emotional well-being.

PANSY: CHEMICAL COMPOSITION AND MEDICINAL PROPERTIES

CHEMICAL COMPOSITION

Pansies, scientifically known as Viola tricolor, contain various compounds that contribute to their medicinal properties.

FLAVONOIDS

Pansies are rich in flavonoids, including rutin, kaempferol, and quercetin. These compounds possess antioxidant properties and contribute to the vibrant colors of the flower.

ANTHOCYANINS

Anthocyanins are responsible for the deep purple, blue, and red pigments found in pansies. These compounds exhibit antioxidant and anti-inflammatory effects.

TANNINS

Tannins are present in pansies and are known for their astringent properties. They contribute to the plant's ability to tone and tighten tissues.

ESSENTIAL OILS

The essential oil extracted from pansies contains various volatile compounds that contribute to its fragrance and potential therapeutic benefits.

MEDICINAL PROPERTIES

Pansies have been traditionally used for their medicinal properties, offering a range of potential health benefits.

ANTIOXIDANT ACTIVITY

The flavonoids and anthocyanins present in pansies exhibit antioxidant activity, helping to protect the body against oxidative stress and free radicals.

ANTI-INFLAMMATORY EFFECTS

Pansies have been used in traditional medicine for their anti-inflammatory properties. These properties may help alleviate inflammation-related conditions and promote overall well-being.

ASTRINGENT AND TONIC ACTIONS

The tannins found in pansies contribute to their astringent properties. Pansies are believed to have toning effects on tissues, making them beneficial for skincare and supporting healthy skin appearance.

TRADITIONAL USES

In traditional medicine, pansies have been used for a variety of purposes, including respiratory support, digestive health, and as a mild diuretic.

It's important to note that while pansies have a history of traditional use for their potential medicinal properties, further scientific research is needed to fully understand and validate these claims. It's always advisable to consult with a healthcare professional before using pansies or any other plant for medicinal purposes.

The chemical composition of pansies and their potential medicinal properties highlight their value as a botanical of interest in traditional medicine and ongoing research endeavors.

PANSY: THERAPEUTIC USES FOR HUMANS

SKIN HEALTH AND BEAUTY

Pansies have been used for various therapeutic purposes related to skin health and beauty.

MOISTURIZING AND SOOTHING

Pansy extracts and preparations are believed to have moisturizing and soothing properties, making them useful in skincare products. They may help hydrate the skin, reduce redness, and calm irritations.

ANTIOXIDANT PROTECTION

The antioxidant compounds found in pansies, such as flavonoids and anthocyanins, may provide protection against oxidative stress and support overall skin health.

TONING AND TIGHTENING

Pansies contain tannins, which have astringent properties. This can contribute to the toning and tightening of skin tissues, promoting a more youthful appearance.

RESPIRATORY SUPPORT

Pansies have been traditionally used to support respiratory health and alleviate certain respiratory conditions.

EXPECTORANT PROPERTIES

Pansies may act as expectorants, helping to loosen and expel mucus from the respiratory tract. This can provide relief from coughs, congestion, and respiratory discomfort.

THROAT SOOTHING

Infusions or gargles made from pansies may have a soothing effect on the throat, helping to alleviate soreness and irritation.

MOOD ENHANCEMENT AND RELAXATION

The delicate fragrance of pansies is often associated with mood enhancement and relaxation.

AROMATHERAPY BENEFITS

Using pansy essential oil in aromatherapy practices, such as through diffusion or massage, may help promote a sense of calm, reduce stress, and enhance relaxation.

OVERALL WELL-BEING

Pansies have been used traditionally for their potential overall health benefits.

ANTIOXIDANT AND ANTI-INFLAMMATORY EFFECTS

The antioxidant and anti-inflammatory properties of pansies may contribute to their potential benefits for overall well-being and supporting a healthy immune system.

TRADITIONAL MEDICINAL USES

In traditional medicine, pansies have been used for digestive health, urinary support, and as a mild diuretic.

While pansies have a history of traditional use for therapeutic purposes, it's important to consult with a healthcare professional before using them for specific health conditions or concerns. Further scientific research is needed to fully understand and validate the therapeutic uses of pansies for humans.

Pansies offer potential benefits for skin health, respiratory support, mood enhancement, and overall well-being, making them a fascinating botanical of interest in various therapeutic applications.

PANSY: THE ROLE OF PANSIES IN MODERN CULTURE

GARDENING AND LANDSCAPING

Pansies play a significant role in modern culture, particularly in the realm of gardening and landscaping.

POPULAR GARDEN PLANT

Pansies are widely cultivated and appreciated as popular garden plants. Their vibrant colors, attractive blooms, and versatility make them a favorite choice for adding beauty and charm to outdoor spaces.

BEDDING PLANTS

Pansies are commonly used as bedding plants, offering a burst of color and visual interest when planted en masse in flower beds or borders. They create stunning displays and contribute to the overall aesthetic appeal of gardens.

CONTAINER PLANTS

Pansies thrive in containers, making them an excellent choice for balcony gardens, patios, and window boxes. Their compact size and ability to withstand cooler temperatures make them versatile plants for container gardening.

FLORAL DESIGN AND CUT FLOWERS

Pansies also play a role in modern floral design and the cut flower industry.

CUT FLOWERS

The vibrant and eye-catching blooms of pansies make them sought-after as cut flowers. They are often used in floral arrangements, bouquets, and centerpieces, adding a touch of charm and color to various occasions and events.

WEDDINGS AND CELEBRATIONS

Pansies are sometimes incorporated into wedding bouquets, corsages, and boutonnieres, symbolizing love, affection, and delicate beauty. Their versatility and wide range of colors make them suitable for different wedding themes and color palettes.

SOCIAL SYMBOLISM

Pansies hold symbolic meanings in modern culture, representing various sentiments and concepts.

THOUGHTFULNESS AND REMEMBRANCE

Pansies are often associated with thoughtfulness and remembrance, making them a fitting choice for sympathy arrangements or as a gesture of care and support.

SYMBOL OF SPRING

Pansies are often seen as a symbol of spring and renewal, signifying the end of winter and the arrival of a new season. They are frequently used in spring-themed decorations and celebrations.

CREATIVE INSPIRATION

The charm and beauty of pansies have inspired various forms of artistic expression.

ART AND DESIGN

Pansies have been depicted in paintings, drawings, and other visual arts, capturing their delicate features and vibrant colors. They serve as subjects for botanical art, nature-inspired designs, and floral motifs in various art forms.

LITERATURE AND POETRY

Pansies have been mentioned in literature and poetry, evoking emotions, symbolism, and metaphors related to their beauty, fragility, and colorful presence.

The role of pansies in modern culture spans gardening, floral design, symbolism, and artistic inspiration, highlighting their enduring appeal and significance in contemporary society.

PANSY: WAYS TO ENJOY AND APPRECIATE THIS PLANT

GARDENING AND LANDSCAPING

One of the primary ways to enjoy and appreciate pansies is through gardening and landscaping activities.

PLANTING IN GARDENS

Plant pansies in your garden beds, borders, or flower patches to create vibrant displays of color. Mix different pansy varieties to add visual interest and create unique combinations.

CONTAINER GARDENING

Grow pansies in containers such as pots, hanging baskets, or window boxes. Place them on balconies, patios, or near windows to enjoy their beauty up close.

VERTICAL GARDENS

Create vertical gardens with pansies by using trellises, wall-mounted planters, or hanging structures. This allows you to make the most of limited space and adds a vertical element to your garden.

FLORAL ARRANGEMENTS

Pansies can be incorporated into various floral arrangements and decorative displays.

BOUQUETS AND CENTERPIECES

Use fresh-cut pansies to create stunning bouquets or centerpieces for special occasions or as decorative accents in your home. Combine them with other compatible flowers to enhance their beauty.

DRIED FLOWER CRAFTS

Dry pansies to preserve their delicate beauty and use them in dried flower crafts. Create wreaths, pressed flower art, or potpourri to enjoy their colors and fragrance for an extended period.

ARTISTIC INSPIRATION

Pansies can serve as inspiration for artistic expression and creative endeavors.

BOTANICAL ART

Create botanical art pieces by painting or drawing pansies. Capture their intricate details and vibrant colors on canvas or paper, showcasing their natural beauty.

PHOTOGRAPHY

Capture the enchanting essence of pansies through photography. Focus on their intricate patterns, textures, and unique color combinations to create visually striking images.

SYMBOLIC SIGNIFICANCE

Pansies hold symbolic meanings that can be appreciated and incorporated into various contexts.

GIFT GIVING

Offer bouquets or potted pansy plants as thoughtful gifts to convey sentiments of love, friendship, or remembrance. The recipient can appreciate the beauty and symbolic value of these flowers.

WEDDINGS AND CELEBRATIONS

Incorporate pansies into wedding bouquets, corsages, or table arrangements to add a touch of elegance and symbolism. Pansies can represent love, beauty, or springtime in these special celebrations.

Whether through gardening, floral arrangements, artistic inspiration, or symbolic gestures, there are numerous ways to enjoy and appreciate the beauty of pansies in your everyday life.

PANSY: CONCLUSION

In conclusion, pansies are remarkable plants that captivate us with their vibrant colors, delicate blooms, and charming presence. They have a rich history, cultural significance, and a wide range of practical uses, making them beloved in gardening, floral design, and various aspects of modern culture.

From their role in garden landscapes to their symbolic meanings in weddings and celebrations, pansies bring joy, beauty, and a sense of renewal. Their versatility allows for creative expressions, whether through art, design, or aromatherapy. Additionally, pansies have been valued for their medicinal properties, culinary uses, and contributions to biodiversity conservation.

As you embark on cultivating pansies, may your journey be filled with delight and success. With proper care, attention to their needs, and appreciation for their unique qualities, you can create stunning displays of color and experience the rewards of nurturing these remarkable plants.

Embrace the beauty of pansies, share their charm with others, and let them inspire your creativity and love for nature. May your gardens bloom with the enchanting allure of pansies, bringing happiness and tranquility to your surroundings.

WISHING YOU A JOYFUL AND SUCCESSFUL
CULTIVATION OF PANSIES!

Made in United States
Troutdale, OR
06/25/2023

10787634R00058